David & Jill Wright

FOCUS ON

FRANCE

Hamish Hamilton · London

To Rachel and Steven

The authors and publishers would like to thank the following for permission to reproduce photographs: Allan Cash Ltd 8, 9, 28 (right); C.M. Dixon 17 (right), 19; Chris Fairclough 1, 11, 14; French Government Tourist Office 16; Robert Harding Picture Library/C. & P. Corrigan 7 (right); The John Hillelson Agency, Elliott Erwitt/Magnum Photos 11, cover; SNCF 23 (left); Spectrum Colour Library 7 (left), 10, 20 (right); Tony Stone Photolibrary-London 6, 17, 20, 24, 25 (right), 27, 29; Topham Picture Library 13, 15. The authors have given permission to reproduce the following photographs: 3, 12, 18, 21, 22 (left and right), 23, 24, 26 (left and right), 28 (left), 31.
Design by Andrew Shoolbred

Map and illustrations by Gary Rees/Linda Rogers Associates

HAMISH HAMILTON CHILDREN'S BOOKS

Published by the Penguin Group
27 Wrights Lane, London W8 5TZ, England
Viking Penguin Inc, 40 West 23rd Street, New York, New York 10010, U.S.A.
Penguin Books Australia Ltd, Ringwood, Victoria, Australia
Penguin Books Canada Ltd, 2801 John Street, Markham, Ontario, Canada L3R 1B4
Penguin Books (N.Z.) Ltd, 182-190 Wairau Road, Auckland 10, New Zealand

Penguin Books Ltd, Registered Offices: Harmondsworth, Middlesex, England

First published in Great Britain 1985 by Hamish Hamilton Children's Books

3 5 7 9 10 8 6 4 2

British Library Cataloguing in Publication Data

Wright, David
Focus on France. – (Focus on)
1. France – Social life and customs – 20th century – Juvenile literature
I. Title II. Wright, Jill
944.083'8 DC33.7

ISBN 0-241-11483-7

Printed in Great Britain by Cambus Litho, East Kilbride, Scotland.

Cover: This could only be France! Notice the straight tree-lined road, the 'baguette' (the long, loaf of bread), and the berets worn by the man and the boy.

Previous page: The centre of Rennes in north-west France. Notice the fine buildings and the cast-iron balconies. There are Citroen and Renault cars with French number plates – '35' is the Département (county) of l'Ille-et-Vilaine. Rennes is the main town of that Département. Notice also the single-deck bus, the cobbled street in the foreground, the shop signs, and the umbrellas (it often rains in north-west France!)

A pleasant valley in the Vosges mountains ▶ in eastern France. Notice the steep hills, covered with pine trees; the fields of pasture in the valley; the little church for the few farmhouses; and the deciduous trees in the valley near the church.

Contents

Introducing France

France is the biggest country in western Europe. It has an area of 547,026 square kilometres, so it is more than twice as big as the United Kingdom or Western Germany, and seventeen times bigger than Belgium.

Fifty-five million people live in France, about the same number as live in the UK. But because France is a much bigger country, it seems a lot less crowded. You can often travel along a country road without seeing any cars or people.

A varied country

France is a varied country. The north and west are mostly lowland, with cool weather for much of the year. The Massif Central is a highland area, with gorges and old volcanoes (see page 27). In the east there are mountains – the Vosges, the Jura and the Alps. The Alps are the highest mountain range in western Europe, and France has western Europe's highest mountain (page 26). The Pyrenees are high mountains, too, on the border with Spain. The south of France is the hottest area, near the Mediterranean Sea.

France is a very interesting and a very beautiful country. In some rural areas, life is still quiet and slow. In the bustling towns and cities, factories and other businesses use ultra-modern equipment and are very efficient.

A changing country

France is changing quickly. The number of people living in villages is going down, and the big towns are growing fast. In some towns of France, there are many Arab immigrants from North Africa, as well as people from Italy, Spain and Portugal. They came because there were good, well-paid jobs in French factories. But now new machines are taking people's jobs, and unemployment has become a problem.

A friendly country

In the past, there were often wars between France and her neighbours. Now they are friendly, and most of these countries belong to the EEC (the European Economic Community, or 'Common Market'). They still argue from time to time, but these arguments are quite small compared with former wars.

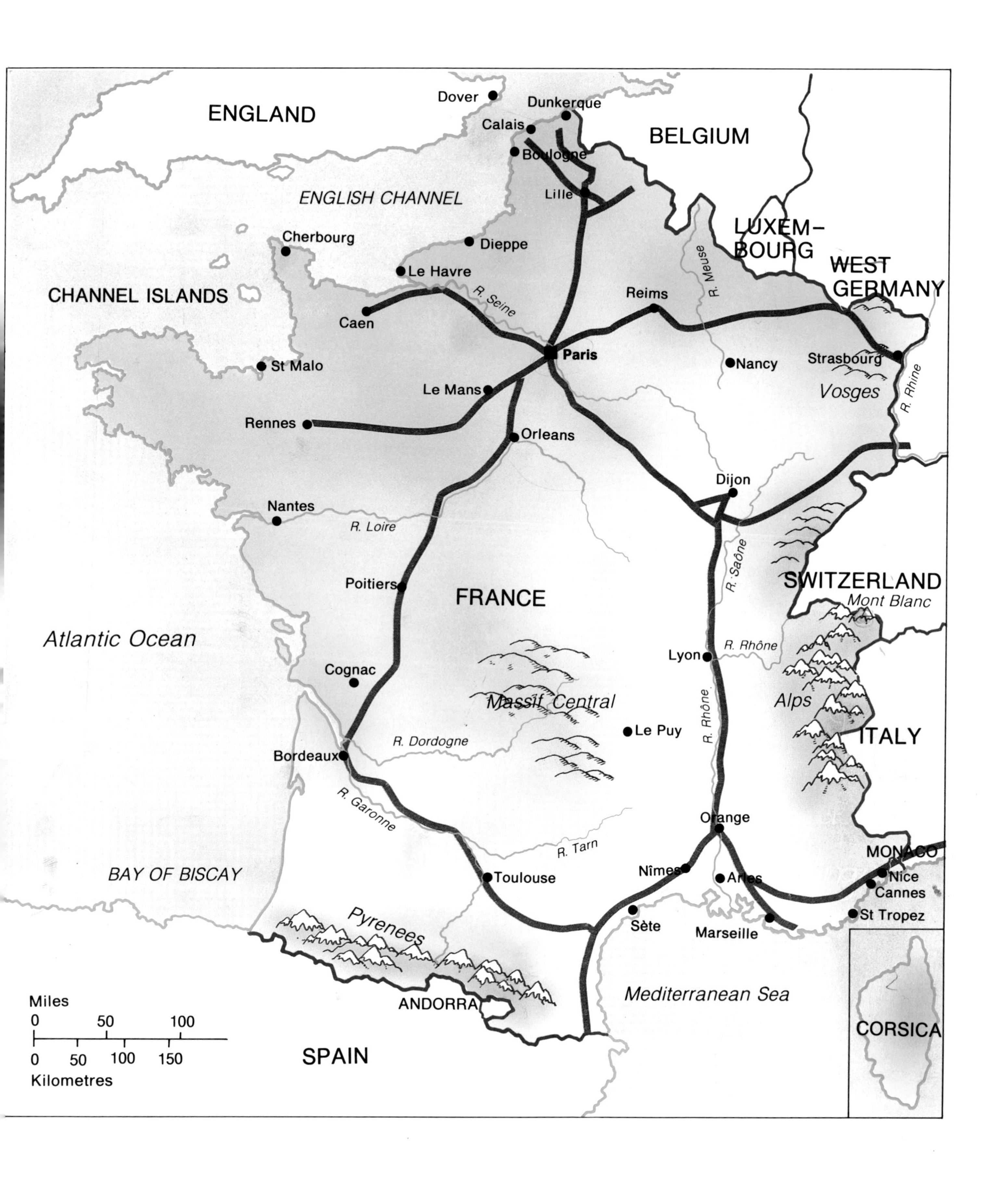

ENGLAND
Dover
Dunkerque
Calais
Boulogne
BELGIUM
ENGLISH CHANNEL
Lille
LUXEM-
BOURG
Cherbourg
Dieppe
R. Meuse
WEST
GERMANY
Le Havre
CHANNEL ISLANDS
Reims
R. Seine
Caen
Paris
St Malo
Nancy
Strasbourg
Le Mans
Vosges
R. Rhine
Rennes
Orleans
Dijon
Nantes
R. Loire
R. Saône
SWITZERLAND
Poitiers
FRANCE
Mont Blanc
Atlantic Ocean
R. Rhône
Lyon
Cognac
Massif Central
Alps
Le Puy
R. Rhône
ITALY
R. Dordogne
Bordeaux
R. Garonne
Orange
R. Tarn
MONACO
BAY OF BISCAY
Nîmes
Arles
Toulouse
Nice
Cannes
Sète
St Tropez
Pyrenees
Marseille
ANDORRA
Mediterranean Sea
Miles
0
50
100
0
50
100
150
Kilometres
SPAIN
CORSICA

Paris

The capital city of France is Paris. Paris is by far the biggest city in France – in fact it is one of the biggest cities in the world. Ten million people live in the Paris region, more than twice the number living in the whole of Norway.

In the capital city

The President of France lives in Paris. 'La République Française' (the French Republic) has a president instead of a king or queen. He is elected every seven years.

The French Parliament always meets in Paris. It has two parts – the National Assembly and the Senate. The National Assembly is elected every five years. Sometimes, the 'Left' has control; sometimes, the 'Right'. The Senate is also elected, but far fewer people can vote for its members.

The best theatres and art galleries, and the headquarters of most industries, are in the capital city, too. And Paris is the headquarters of UNESCO – the United Nations Educational, Scientific and Cultural Organisation. Paris is always crowded with politicians, tourists, businessmen, stage-stars and many other visitors.

The centre of Paris

Paris started on an island in the River Seine. This was a safe place when there were wars or rebellions. Today, the 'Île de la Cité' (Island of the City) is still the centre of Paris. The great cathedral of Notre Dame is on the Île de la Cité: look for the two big towers in the photograph below. 'Notre Dame' means 'Our Lady' (the Virgin Mary, mother of Jesus). Many people come to this cathedral to worship God, or simply to admire the architecture. The cathedral has stood there for seven hundred years, and has survived several French revolutions and two world wars.

Notre Dame cathedral and the River Seine, with a boat full of tourists.

Other famous buildings

The Arc de Triomphe (Triumphal Arch) celebrates the victories of Emperor Napoleon. Between 1800 and 1812 he conquered most of Europe. His victories are listed on the walls (they do not list his defeats!).

The Arc de Triomphe. Twelve big roads meet here at the world's busiest roundabout.

The Eiffel Tower celebrates a different kind of victory – the victory of science and engineering. It was built for a great exhibition in 1889. At that time, it was the tallest building in the world. It is 300 metres high, and weighs 7000 tonnes. There is a superb view of Paris from the top.

The Sacré Coeur (Sacred Heart) is a church built on a hill in the part of Paris known as Montmartre. Its gleaming white domes are made of limestone. It looks much older than the Eiffel Tower, but was built at about the same time.

A growing city

Paris is getting bigger. For years it grew upwards, with high blocks of flats and offices. Now no more high buildings are allowed in the central area: the government does not want the historic buildings to be dwarfed by any more skyscrapers. Instead, five big New Towns are being built, complete with houses, flats, offices and factories.

Many of the people who live in these towns work in the capital. Cergy-Pointoise New Town has double-decker trains going to and from the centre of Paris because single-deck trains cannot cope with all the commuters.

A new town: flats at Marne la Vallée.

Towns

The biggest cities

Most French people live in towns or cities. Paris is by far the biggest city with ten million inhabitants. Two other cities have over a million people each. Lyon, in south-east France, is the second-biggest city. It is built where the River Saône meets the River Rhône. Lyon has preserved many of its traditional cobbled streets and quaint old houses. But its wealth is now based on industry.

Marseille is almost as big as Lyon. It is the main French port on the Mediterranean Sea, quite near the delta of the River Rhône. It is a big industrial city, not a seaside resort. The tourist towns of Cannes and Nice are east of Marseille.

Lille will soon have over a million people, too. This town is in the north-east, near Belgium, and was once a big coal-mining town. North-east France has many mining and industrial towns which almost join one another. Now, most of the coal-mines have closed down, although there are still lots of factories in the area.

There are hundreds of other towns in France. Most grew up as market-towns to serve the surrounding countryside. Ports have grown up at the coast: Bordeaux and Le Havre (The Harbour) are among the largest.

What are French towns like?

Every town is different. Yet there are some features which you will find in nearly all French towns. For example in the centre there is often a large square, sometimes called 'La Place'. It is often the site of a colourful daily or weekly market. It also usually contains a big building labelled 'Hôtel de Ville' (Town Hall), or 'Mairie' (Mayor's Office). The

The town square at Auray, N.W. France.

French flag flies there to show that the mayor is loyal to his country. The square and the boulevards often have trees to give shade. Sometimes the trees are cut to a square shape to match the shape of the buildings.

The most useful building for visitors is the 'syndicat d'initiatives' (the tourist office). Here you will be given free maps, free leaflets, and free advice on a hotel or 'pension' (guest house) or 'auberge de jeunesse' (youth hostel) to stay the night. France looks after visitors well.

Most towns have many places of interest. Some were founded by the Romans and have important Roman remains, like the amphitheatre at Arles. But some towns in northern France were badly damaged in the two world wars and have been almost completely rebuilt. They now look very new.

Where do people live?

Many people in France live in flats. Each block of flats is usually well looked after by a caretaker. In most flats, big doors open onto a balcony, where there may be colourful window-boxes filled with flowers. On the edge of all big towns, there are huge blocks of modern 'HLM' flats ('habitations à loyers modérés', meaning 'homes at moderate rent'). The government has spent a lot of money building these flats to try and ease the widespread housing problem.

In France, fewer people own their own homes than in Britain or America. But nowadays, more and more new houses in the suburbs are being offered for sale. Some richer people with a flat in town also have a country cottage to visit at weekends.

Everywhere in France windows have shutters. Shutters stop the sun coming in, but allow the air to circulate. Most windows open inwards so that people can open and close the shutters with ease. Even houses in Calais and Boulogne have shutters, although just across the Channel, where the climate is exactly the same, English houses have none.

A narrow street with old houses at Florac in southern France. Notice the wooden shutters.

Shops

Shopping in France

Many shops in France are quite small and have been owned by the same families for many years. The shops stay open much later than in most other countries in northern Europe, and the shopkeepers work very hard. However, shops sometimes close for two or three hours in the middle of the day; and many shops shut completely for two or three weeks in July or August while the owners are away on holiday.

You will notice many differences if you go shopping in France. When you shop for food, you have to buy milk in a carton, not a bottle – the milk is 'homogenised', with no cream at the top. If you buy meat, you could choose horse-meat – this is popular in France. But meat at the 'boucherie' (the butcher) is expensive, so you might go to a 'charcuterie' instead – the cooked-meat shop. Here, there are lots of different types of pâté, cold meat and sausage.

For groceries it is simplest to go to an 'épicerie' (a grocer) labelled 'libre service'. Here you can choose the goods for yourself and pay at the exit. And don't be alarmed at finding a shop labelled 'poissonerie' – it's only a fish shop!

Cakes and pastries for sale at a pâtisserie.

The markets

Nearly every town has a market. Large towns have a market every day – the biggest have several markets, some of which concentrate on one type of produce, such as flowers. Paris has a 'flea market', though there aren't any fleas for sale! It sells antiques, which have become very popular.

Small towns have a market once a week. In the past, local products were the main items on the stalls. But nowadays it is as easy to buy peaches and oranges in the north of France as in the south. Some market traders use

Locally-grown vegetables being sold at a market in central France.

their lorries as market stalls: they simply open up one side and display their goods in the lorry. Each day they travel to another market in a different town.

Hypermarkets

In France, huge 'hypermarchés' were built at the edge of towns long before they appeared in Britain. A hypermarket is a complete shopping-centre under one roof, with lots of giant bargain-packs and special offers. The bargains are so good that people drive a long way to shop at the hypermarket. Some people from England even make special shopping-trips to visit the hypermarkets at the Channel ports. But many French people like the old shops, and are worried that hypermarkets may put some of the small shops out of business.

French money

When you buy something in France, you pay for it in francs. Look at a newspaper to find out what the franc is worth. How many francs would you get for your weekly pocket-money?

There are 100 centimes in one franc. One centime is now too small to be of any use. Even the little 5 centime coins are becoming quite rare. The 10, 20 and 50 centime coins are gold-coloured, and the 1, 2 and 5 franc coins are silver-coloured. You can see some of them below. The biggest coin is the 10 franc coin. For bigger amounts of money there are bank notes.

Here are some of the more common shop signs:

boucherie	*butcher*
boulangerie	*baker*
charcuterie	*cold meats*
épicerie	*grocer*
librairie	*bookshop*
pâtisserie	*pastries and cakes*
pharmacie	*chemist*
poissonerie	*fishmonger*
quincaillerie	*hardware*

Farming

France has more farmland than any other country in western Europe, so farmers are very important in France. If you flew over northern France in an aeroplane, you would look down on a scene like the one shown below. There are very few hedges, so the crops stretch as far as you can see. The different crops make a beautiful pattern because they are grown on land which is divided into small strips.

Nowadays, French farmers have tractors, combine harvesters and other machinery, so it is very difficult to farm these narrow strip-fields. The government is trying to rearrange the strips so that the farmers have fewer, bigger fields. You can see some bigger fields at the top of the photograph (below left). The gold-coloured fields in the photograph are growing wheat, barley and maize (sweet corn). The green fields have grass or sugar-beet. These are the main crops in the north.

Some parts of France do not have open fields like this. In parts of the west there are more hedges, and more of the land is used for grass and fodder crops for cattle.

Strip-fields in northern France.

What are the crops used for?

Most of the wheat is used for bread. French bread is especially tasty: the crust is very crisp, and the inside is light and airy. But after only a day it is stale and tough. French people like to live near a boulangerie so that they can buy fresh bread before breakfast each morning, and sometimes in the evening before dinner, too.

Most of the barley and maize is fed to animals. The tops of the sugar-beet are also used for animal food. The beet is used to make white sugar.

French bread, fresh from the baker.

The farmer's problems

Farmers with a lot of land have few problems – except when it rains too little or too much. But most farmers in France do not own much land, and they have a great many problems. For example, they cannot afford large, new machines to cultivate the soil. And they say that the price they receive for their crops or fruit is not high enough, even though the Common Market tries to help small farmers by raising prices for farm products higher than anywhere else in the world. Sometimes, French farmers use their tractors to block the roads in protest at what they think are low prices. If they consider the price very low, they may tip their crops all over the road.

Where does fruit grow?

Fruit growing is very important in many parts of France. In the cooler north-west, apples are the main fruit crop. Some are used to make cider, especially in Normandy. The south is better suited to fruit such as peaches, apricots and oranges. They ripen in the hot sun and are sent to other parts of France, as well as to other countries in Europe.

Pears grow well in both north and south France. Find out if your local greengrocer sells French fruit. If he does, ask him if he can spare a label from one of the boxes. See how many things you can find out about the fruit.

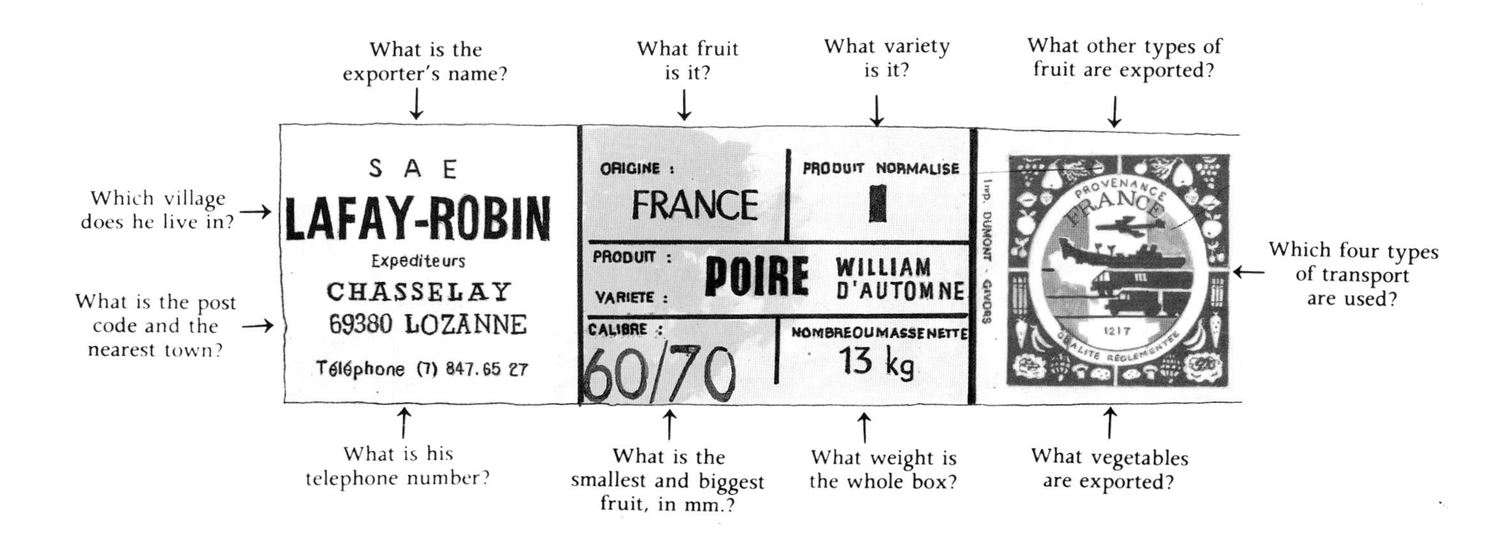

Cheese and wine

France is famous throughout the world for its cheeses and wines. Some people collect the labels from cheeses or from wine bottles, and discover where each label comes from.

Why are cheeses different?

There are hundreds of varieties of cheese in France. Each type of cheese is only made in one small part of France, although some are sold to many different countries.

There are several reasons why cheeses vary: different climates; different grass; different animals; different amounts of time taken in making the cheese; and different methods of making cheese. The last two reasons are the most important. Most French cheeses are made in small factories, using secret methods that no-one can copy.

Some well-known cheeses

Brie is a big round white soft cheese. Usually, you only buy part of a whole Brie – they measure 35 centimetres across! Brie cheeses come from an area of a wet clay lowland to the south of Paris where the grass is very lush.

Camembert is a smaller round cheese with a hard white outside and a soft pale yellow inside. It is normally sold in a round wooden box. Camembert comes from the grasslands of Normandy, near Caen and Rouen.

Some French cheeses are not made from cows' milk. Roquefort, for example, is made from sheep's milk. The sheep live on the dry grasslands of the Massif Central. The cheeses are stored in the local limestone caves until they are ripe.

There are lots of goat cheeses too. The one shown below is a soft cheese. It is sold in a tub with two goats drawn on it.

Brie cheese (left); fresh goat cheese; and Camembert cheese (right).

The grape harvest time in St Guiroud, southern France.

France's vineyards

Grapes can grow in most parts of France, except in the mountains and in the far north-west where it is too cool. But the best grapes grow on sunny, south-facing slopes. Fortunately, vines do not need a particularly rich soil.

Most wine is made near where the grapes are grown. White wine can be made from white or red grapes. A machine removes the stalks and crushes the grapes. Then the grape-juice is strained off and fermented. Red wine is made just from red grapes.

Some special wines are named after towns or regions of France, such as Bordeaux, Chablis and Champagne. Cognac is the name of a town which has become the name of a brandy.

The vine-grower's problems

One big problem is that disease or insect pests can destroy the crops. To avoid this, farmers have to spray the vines with insecticide each year.

Another problem is the weather, which has a big effect on the quality of the wine. When the weather is good the vines produce grapes that make a particularly fine wine. That year is then called a 'vintage' year. But there are many poor years when the wine is less good. The vine-grower may lose a lot of money. French vine-growers are also worried about the import of cheaper wine from Spain, Italy, and Algeria (in North Africa).

Who drinks French wine?

Most people in France drink wine. Even young children are allowed a little wine in a glass of water. Some people drink too much wine, so you can often see posters saying 'Santé: Sobriété' (Health: Sobriety), and notices headed, 'Suppression de l'ivresse publique' (Prevention of public drunkenness).

A large section of every French supermarket sells bottles of wine. There are hundreds of different types and prices. 'Vin ordinaire' (ordinary wine) for everyday meals is very cheap. Vintage wines are more expensive. Many are exported abroad. French wines are thought to be the best in the world.

Food

France is famous throughout the world for its good food and cuisine. ('Cuisine' is the French word for 'cooking'.) French people take a great interest in food and know a lot about the preparation and cooking of it. It is normal for a family to spend a quarter of its income on buying food or eating out in restaurants.

Lunch at a hotel in Coulans, near Le Mans. The basket of fresh bread is always kept full.

Breakfast

Breakfast in France is a simple meal – usually coffee with French bread or croissants, sometimes with butter or jam. Children sometimes prefer 'pain au chocolat'. This is a kind of bread roll with soft chocolate inside. A lot of people eat breakfast in a café on their way to work. They usually stand up to eat because most cafés charge more for sitting down.

Lunch or supper

In towns, lunch or supper is often eaten in a café or restaurant. Even the smallest café produces tasty, well-cooked meals, often at a very reasonable price. If you choose the 'menu prix fixe' ('fixed price menu'), you get a three-course meal and a glass of wine for a special low price. But there is usually only a choice of one or two dishes per course.

The first course may consist of soup, often with lots of vegetables chopped up in it, pâté, or an 'hors d'oeuvres', which may include a dozen salad vegetables.

Cooked vegetables are often eaten before the meat or fish, although the same plate and the same knife and fork are used for both dishes. Meat and vegetables are only cooked until they are just tender. The French do not like overcooked food.

After the main course, there is usually a choice of French cheeses.

Today's menu: Fillet of sea bream (a kind of fish); Rabbit with peppers; and Turkey escalope in breadcrumbs.

Many people round off a meal with a 'digestif'. This is a drink which is supposed to help you digest your food. Some 'digestifs' are brightly coloured.

Regional specialities

All over France, restaurants serve hundreds of different types of food – including frogs' legs and edible snails! Each region usually has its own speciality. Near the coast there are spécialités de la mer' – fish and shell fish. In Burgundy, there is 'coq au vin' – chicken cooked in wine.

Some regional foods can now be bought all over France and abroad too. 'Crêpes' used to be a speciality of Brittany, in the far west. Today, these big, but deliciously thin pancakes are popular almost everywhere. 'Quiches Lorraine' orginally came from Lorraine, in eastern France. Now these open tarts, filled with egg, onion and bacon, are eaten in many different countries.

Cooking crêpes in Brittany. Customers can choose from many different fillings.

Changing habits

Eating habits are changing. For example, most towns have a 'self' – a fast-food café, more like an American café, than a French restaurant. Even the name is American: it is short for 'self-service'. People who like traditional French food say that the food in these cafés is tasteless and boring. But those in a hurry like being able to have a quick, convenient meal.

Power and industry

The 10 franc coin has the highest value of all French coins, and it shows the most important French products: power and industry. (You can see pylons and cranes on the coin.) France is a major industrial country, but it faces serious problems because it does not have enough coal, and it has hardly any oil. Most of the power has to be imported, and this is very expensive. France imports over half the coal she needs, three-quarters of the gas, and nearly all the oil.

Most of France's coal-mines were in the north, near the border with Belgium. But many mines have closed down in the last twenty years because the best coal has been dug out, and the narrow seams of coal that remain are too expensive to mine. Fortunately, the Common Market makes it easier for France to import coal from Germany.

Other sources of power

Hydro-electric power (HEP for short) is one source of power. It is produced in the mountains where the rivers are dammed. The highest mountains – the Alps and Pyrenees – produce the largest amount of HEP.

Tidal power is another type of water power. A dam has been built across the River Rance, near St Malo, so that when the tide comes in or goes out, the water drives turbines to make electricity. This was the first big scheme for tidal power in the world.

The tidal power dam on the River Rance, near St Malo. In the background, you can see the pylons for the electric cables.

Made in France

France has to spend so much money importing coal and oil, that she has to export lots of goods to replace it. Almost every type of shop in your country sells some French-made goods. And almost every home contains some French products. For example –

- this book was first written with a BIC ball-point pen from France
- my omelette was prepared in a Moulinex mixer and cooked in a Le Creuset frying-pan from France
- the glasses on the table were made by Arcoroc and came from France
- my bathroom cabinet is made in France by Alibert
- lots of my children's toys are French-made, such as Majorette toy cars, and modern Meccano

Important industries

One of the most important industries in France is making cars. Nearly three million cars are made each year. They have badges to show what make they are –

Citroen make the car that Maigret, the famous detective, used. They make big luxury cars, and also cheap runabouts such as the 2CV.

The Citroen car factory at Rennes.

CV stands for CheVal (horse); and it was called the 2CV because it was only as powerful as two horses. Nowadays people prefer the 6CV.

Renault is government-owned. There are so many Renaults made in the big factory near Paris that whole trains and huge barges are used to transport them.

Peugeot is now part of the Talbot group. Their estate cars are especially popular. Large French families find the version with three rows of seats very useful.

At Toulouse, in the south, there is a big aircraft factory. Some of the supersonic Concorde aircraft were made here. France makes and sells aircraft to airlines and airforces in many parts of the world.

Rivers and canals

The great rivers of France

France is fortunate in having many long, wide rivers. For hundreds of years they have been important for transport. In recent years, they have lost some of their importance to railways and roads, but there are still thousands of large barges which travel the rivers. And big, modern locks have been built to make some rivers even more useful than before.

The rivers of France are beautiful as well as useful. The French Impressionist painters often painted peaceful river scenes. Many rivers have lines of poplar trees along their bank, which give alternate sun and shade.

The River Seine is used by many barges; if you stand on a bridge in Paris, a pair of barges will go under you every few minutes. From Paris the River Seine flows in a meandering route westwards to the Channel.

The River Loire flows westwards to the Atlantic, but it is not such a busy river as the Seine. There are fewer big towns on its banks, and the current is fast. Many people think it is the most beautiful river in France.

An Impressionist painting by Monet, *The River*.

The River Loire near Chambord.

The River Rhine forms part of the boundary between France and Germany. The Rhine is an international river, starting in Switzerland and ending in the Netherlands. Barges on this river can travel between the inland ports of many countries.

The only large river that flows south to the Mediterranean is the River Rhône. Most rivers in southern France are almost dry in the hot summer. But the Rhône comes from a glacier in Switzerland and collects water from many mountain streams so there is plenty of water all year round.

The Rhône has many uses: its water irrigates fields; it produces hydro-electricity; and it is used for transport.

These rivers, and some others, are linked together by canals, which make them more useful for navigation.

Canals

Almost all the canals in France are in the northern half of the country. One exception is the Canal du Midi (Canal of the South), which links Bordeaux, near the Atlantic Ocean, with Sète, on the Mediterranean Sea. Yet this canal is too narrow to be very useful. There is a plan to make it wider and deeper, but carrying it out would be very expensive.

In the northern half of France, the main items carried by canal are heavy 'raw materials' which are used in industry – coal and oil for power; iron ore for making steel; sand, gravel and cement for building houses and factories.

A big barge near Reims, on the Aisne-Marne Canal. Notice the car and the washing line!

Whole families live on the huge barges that carry these goods. The parents park their car on the barge and hang their washing outside. It dries well as the barge goes along. Very young children play in a playpen to keep them safe. When the barge carries sand, children have a huge travelling sandpit to keep them happy!

Water transport is good because the barges can take big loads, they use up less petrol than lorries, and they keep lorries off the roads. As a result, there is less danger, less pollution, and traffic jams are less frequent. But barges are slow, especially at locks. The big locks on the Rhine canal hold four big boats, so they can all move together when the lock gates open.

Roads and railways

Roads

More and more cars and lorries are using the roads of France. Lots of 'A' roads (motorways) are being built. You have to pay to use most of these motorways. When you join a motorway, you collect a card. Then, when you leave the motorway, you have to stop and pay. The farther you travel, the more you pay.

The busiest motorway of all is the 'autoroute périphérique' which encircles Paris. On Friday evenings, there is so much traffic that it moves very slowly indeed. The A7 motorway to the south is very busy too. French holiday-makers and tourists use it to reach the Mediterranean coast, and many lorries travel along it from Paris to the large towns of the south.

Motorway junction near Orly airport, south of Paris.

Many quiet French roads are lined with poplar trees.

Most French roads are not 'A' roads or 'N' (national) roads. The majority are quiet 'D' roads (departmental roads) that go through attractive countryside and link villages and small towns. Most of them run between long avenues of poplar trees. Some are very straight; these are usually old Roman roads still in use after two thousand years.

Railways

France is very proud of its railways, and the government spends a great deal of money building new trains and railways. A few years ago, millions of francs were spent in building a brand-new railway for the most important route in France: from Paris to Lyon. This new fast route is more direct than the old one, with no tight bends to slow the train down. In fact, the train travels so fast that in 1981 it broke the record for the world's fastest train. It is called the TGV (Train à Grande Vitesse). It is a superb train to travel in – smooth and comfortable.

Freight trains and other passenger trains still use the old railway. These trains have powerful electric engines which travel faster than most trains in other countries, though not as fast as the TGV. There are lots of other express trains too, called Turbotrains or TEE's.

The TGV at Lyon station, at the start of its fast journey to Paris.

The little trains that travel more slowly through the countryside, stopping at village stations, are very useful too. Many branch-line railways are still open. Some of the old red and white railcars that used to travel on the branch-lines had the driver's cab above roof level, so that passengers could sit at the very front of the train. But these are being replaced with more modern railcars.

A modern SNCF diesel railcar at St Dié, in the Vosges mountains. Notice the low platforms, typical of French railway stations.

What do the letters mean?

SNCF — Société Nationale des Chemins de Fer Français
National Society of 'roads of iron' (railways) of France

TGV — Train à Grande Vitesse
Train 'at great speed' (high-speed train)

TEE — Trans Europ Express
Trans European Express

The coasts of France

France is a fortunate country because it has a coastline on three sides: in the north, there is the English Channel ('la Manche'); in the west, the Atlantic Ocean; and in the south the Mediterranean Sea. Each of these coastlines is very different from the others.

The high chalk cliffs at Étretat.

The coast of 'La Manche'

Most tourists from England cross la Manche by the shortest route. They travel by ferry-boat or hovercraft to either Calais or Boulogne. It is also possible to travel to Dunkerque (a large port near the Belgian border) or to Dieppe (north of Rouen). Longer journeys – sometimes by overnight ship – can take you from England to Cherbourg, St Malo or Roscoff.

The coast of la Manche is often cold, windy and wet in winter. But there are lots of seaside towns. In summer, many French people, and some from England, visit them for a holiday. Between the seaside towns there are high cliffs along many parts of the coast. The chalk cliffs at Étretat have been eroded into arches and stacks. There are fishing-harbours, too. Fishermen go to the North Sea and the Atlantic, and return with fish for the local markets and shops as well as for the rest of France.

Brittany

Brittany, in the far north-west, is very different from the rest of France. The cliffs are made of granite – a hard rock that was once molten, and cooled down deep in the earth. There are lovely bays and islands, and rock-pools on the shore. Fishermen catch crabs and lobsters as well as fish. Some of the people still speak Breton, a language rather like Welsh. The Breton place-names are similar to place-names in Cornwall because the Cornish language was also similar to Breton.

The rocky coastline near Ploumanach, Brittany.

The far west of Brittany is very stormy, but there are good harbours. This area is called Finistère. It means 'Land's End', and it looks rather like Land's End in Cornwall.

The Atlantic Coast

Most of the Atlantic coast of France has long sandy beaches and shallow sea. The area called Les Landes to the south of Bordeaux, has very high sand-dunes, most of which have now been planted with pine trees. This is a good place for a beach holiday – except when the wind blows the fine sand. The big Atlantic waves are superb for surfing, although they can also be dangerous. Bordeaux is an important French port, despite being a long way from the open sea.

The Mediterranean Coast

The Mediterranean is the most popular coast. It is warm in winter and hot in summer. The sea has hardly any tide.

There are many famous resorts along the coast, especially east of the Rhône delta. St Tropez, Cannes and Nice have attracted tourists for more than a century. This part of the Mediterranean coast has become rather crowded, and new tourist resorts for sunbathing, swimming and boating have been built to the west of the Rhône delta.

Yet there are still peaceful parts. The Rhône Delta itself has a nature reserve, famous for its flamingoes.

Sadly the beauty of the coast is marred by pollution of the sea. Fewer fish live in the Mediterranean now, and in some places the water is becoming unsafe even for bathing. It is a problem that no-one has yet solved.

The Mediterranean coast at Cannes.

Mountains

The Alps and Pyrenees

Mont Blanc (White Mountain) is the highest mountain in western Europe. It is on the border of France and Italy.

People can travel from one country to the other by cable-car, or through the Mont Blanc tunnel. The peak is 4807 metres high, while many other mountains in the French Alps are over 3000 metres high.

Along the border with Spain is another range of mountains, the Pyrenees. Some peaks here also reach over 3000 metres. The Alps and the Pyrenees are similar in some ways. They are both very high ranges of mountains and they were both made by folding of the rocks. Layers of rock which collected beneath the sea were slowly squeezed and squeezed until they were forced upwards into high ridges of rocks.

The Col du Tourmalet in the Pyrenees.

For millions of years, as the rocks were forced upwards, they were being worn away by water and weather. In the Ice Ages, glaciers dug the valleys deeper and frost broke rocks high on the mountain-sides. Now the valleys have very steep sides and many mountain peaks are pointed and jagged. There are still some glaciers in the Alps, such as the Mer de Glace (Sea of Ice) on the slopes of Mont Blanc.

The Massif Central

The Massif Central is an area of very old rocks, much older than the Alps or the Pyrenees. These rocks have been eroded for a long time. Farming is difficult here and some villages have been deserted. But now some parts of the Massif Central are trying to attract tourists. Valleys have been dammed to make lakes for sailing. The lakes have sandy beaches, even though the Massif Central is a long way from the sea.

There are some spectacular tourist attractions in some parts of this area. In the north, old volcanoes have been eroded so that only the hard central core remains, as a great natural tower. At Le Puy, a church has been built on top of one of these peaks.

In the west there is limestone country. Between the dry, rocky uplands are beautiful, deep gorges. The gorges of the River Tarn are famous, and a canoe journey through them is very exciting. Underneath the limestone hills there are lots of caves, with beautiful stalactites and stalagmites. La Grande Stalagmite in the Aven Armand cave is the tallest in the world. Prehistoric people once lived in some of the caves, and they have left wonderful rock paintings.

Le Puy, in the Massif Central.

Other mountain ranges

There are two other mountainous areas in the east of France. The Vosges overlook the River Rhine and the border with Germany. The Jura are on the border with part of Switzerland. The highest points are over 1400 metres, yet they are not dramatic mountains like the Alps or rugged like the Massif Central. Both the Vosges and the Jura are mainly forested with pine trees. They are beautiful areas and many French people enjoy holidays in these mountains.

Corsica is a mountainous island in the Mediterranean Sea, near Italy. The highest mountains here reach nearly 3000 metres – twice as high as Ben Nevis, and higher than the Vosges, Jura, or the Massif Central.

Exploring the past

Prehistoric remains

By far the oldest man-made sites in France are the stone-age cave paintings. Some of these paintings are said to be 40,000 years old! The best place to find them is in the Dordogne, to the west of the Massif Central. Many of the paintings show hunting scenes.

The standing-stones of Brittany are over 4000 years old. They are called menhirs. There are hundreds of them. Some are tall and clearly seen from far away. At Carnac, in southern Brittany, there are several long lines of menhirs. No-one knows exactly why they are placed upright, but it was almost certainly something to do with the religion of the people.

A standing-stone in a farmer's field, Brittany.

Le Pont du Gard, the great Roman aqueduct near Nîmes.

The Romans

Two thousand years ago, the Romans created many fine buildings, mainly in the south of France. The temple, the amphitheatre and the aqueduct at Nîmes are the finest remains of all. The Roman triumphal arch at Orange is still standing, too. They must have been very well built to survive for so long.

The Middle Ages

The finest buildings of the Middle Ages are the churches, abbeys and cathedrals. Mont St Michel is one of the most interesting abbeys. It is built on a steep granite island in the sea, on the boundary between Brittany and Normandy. Pilgrims and tourists have to climb a steep cobbled road to reach the great abbey church at the top.

Every great French city has a beautiful cathedral. Perhaps the most beautiful of all is Chartres near Paris. The rose-window has some of the finest stained glass in the world. Even today, the church or cathedral is the tallest building in many towns – yet many big churches are over five hundred years old.

The châteaux

France has thousands of châteaux. These are stately homes. Many are now open to visitors. The oldest châteaux are like castles, and were built to be easily defended during wars and riots. Many have moats round them. When France became more peaceful, the towers and moats were less necessary, so later châteaux have smaller towers and bigger windows. Historians can judge the age of the château by looking at its design.

In the French Revolution of 1789, the poor people attacked some of the châteaux because they felt it was unfair that some people were so rich, while many people went hungry. So there are a number of ruined châteaux in France. But many are well-preserved and are still lived in. The valley of the Loire has many beautiful examples. Some of them are lived in by people who own the famous vineyards of the Loire. These châteaux are shown on the labels of bottles of wine produced by these vine-growers. Tourists may spend their entire holiday visiting the châteaux.

The château at Azey-le-Rideau is surrounded by a moat. The château is 25 km south-west of Tours, near the Loire valley. It was built between 1518 and 1529. It has bigger windows and smaller towers than older châteaux.

France and the world

The EEC

France is one of the six founder members of the EEC (European Economic Community, or Common Market). The Community grew out of the ECSC (European Coal and Steel Community) which was set up after the end of the Second World War in 1945. France and Germany had been in terrible wars three times in seventy-five years, and it was hoped that if they shared their coal and iron, they would not fight each other again. And, in fact, this has been the case. There have been no wars in Europe for forty years, twice as long as the time between the two world wars (1919–39).

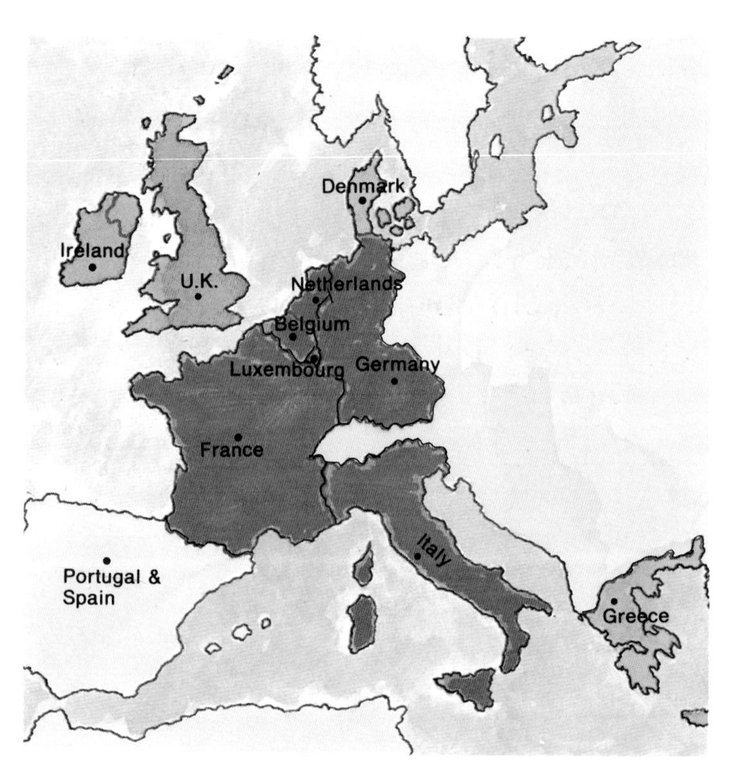

In 1957, the EEC was formed. This was another step forward. The first six members are shown in the darkest colour on the map. Then the UK, Ireland and Denmark joined in 1973. Most people in Western Europe are now in the EEC.

The main advantage of belonging to the EEC is that exports and imports are easier to arrange. This is because there are no extra payments at the frontiers. Factories and businesses benefit, as do their customers, since there is a wider choice of goods in the shops.

Another advantage is that people are free to find jobs anywhere in the Common Market. If you live in one of the member countries there are ten countries where you can work.

The parliament of the EEC sometimes meets in Luxembourg and at other times in Strasbourg. Strasbourg is in eastern France, near the border with Germany. Each member country sends Euro MP's to represent its views and to work out the best policy for the whole community.

France in the world

Street market at Pointe-à-Pitre, Guadeloupe.

The stamp on the left is French, and has a Paris postmark. But there are banana palms on the left, and coconut palms on the right. At the front there are tropical ferns and other plants that cannot grow in France. Why?

The other stamp is also French. Yet there is a dug-out canoe in the picture – and more coconut palms. Why?

The answer is that some islands in the hot tropics belong to France – in fact they are part of France. They use French stamps, so some French stamps show these beautiful islands. The first stamp shows the island of Guadeloupe; the second shows the island of Martinique. Both are in the West Indies. They were captured by the French long ago to grow tropical crops like sugar and tobacco.

Nowadays, the people who live here use French coins and stamps and elect a member to the French Parliament, although their way of life is very different from that of most people in France. Look at the photograph of the street market in the main town of Guadeloupe. It is quite unlike most French markets.

Many other parts of the world used to be owned by France. The African countries have gained their independence, but nearly half of all countries in Africa still have French as their official language. The French-speaking countries of Africa cover a much greater area than France, and they continue to co-operate with the country which once ruled them. Africa needs France for advice and machinery, and doctors and teachers; France needs Africa for tropical crops and minerals. Many people from Africa (especially from North Africa) and from the West Indies have come to live in France to find jobs. So France contains many people who have moved away from their original home.

One and a half million French people live abroad. Many of them will return home in a few years, but others will take their places. And one and a half million people working in France are not French. Some of them, too, will return home. But many want to stay in France, and some of their children already feel French.

Index and summary

Area:	547,026 square kilometres
Population:	54,414,000 (approx.)
Capital:	Paris
Main towns:	Lyon, Marseille, Lille, Bordeaux, Toulouse, Nantes, Nice
Main exports:	Machinery, vehicles, chemicals, foodstuffs
Main imports:	Coal, oil
Main crops:	Wheat, barley, vines, sugar-beet, fruit
Highest point:	Mont Blanc, 4807 metres
Longest river:	the Loire
Official language:	French
Currency:	100 centimes to 1 franc
National airline:	Air France